FOR MY DAUGHTER, ALLIE.

Written by Lori Nachtigal Rothschild, MS, CCC–SLP

facebook.com/slpfeedingtherapy/

@speechandfeedingadvice

Illustrated by Alexandra Feder
Designed by Amber Harris

Printed in the United States of America

ISBN-13: 978-0692998458
ISBN-10: 0692998458

First Printing, 2017

Picky Patty only liked to eat pizza.

Pizza on Monday.
Pizza on Tuesday.
Pizza on Wednesday, Thursday, and Friday.

One Saturday, Mommy said
"Try some chicken, please."

"Just take a lick, Patty."

"NO CHICKY!"
cried Picky Patty.

"Okay, Patty, then let's play a game.
Watch Mommy put on chicky lipstick."

"NO CHICKY LIPSTICK!"
cried Picky Patty.

CHOP! CHOP!

"Okay, Patty. Then chicky chicky chopsticks."

"NO CHICKY CHICKY CHOPSTICKS!"
cried Picky Patty.

"Okay, Patty, then chicky chicky,
dip dip, lick lick" said Mommy.

"Patty do! Patty do! Mmm..." said Patty.

HOORAY!

"Great job, Patty!" said Mommy.

"Now watch mommy's chicky magic make the chicken disappear."

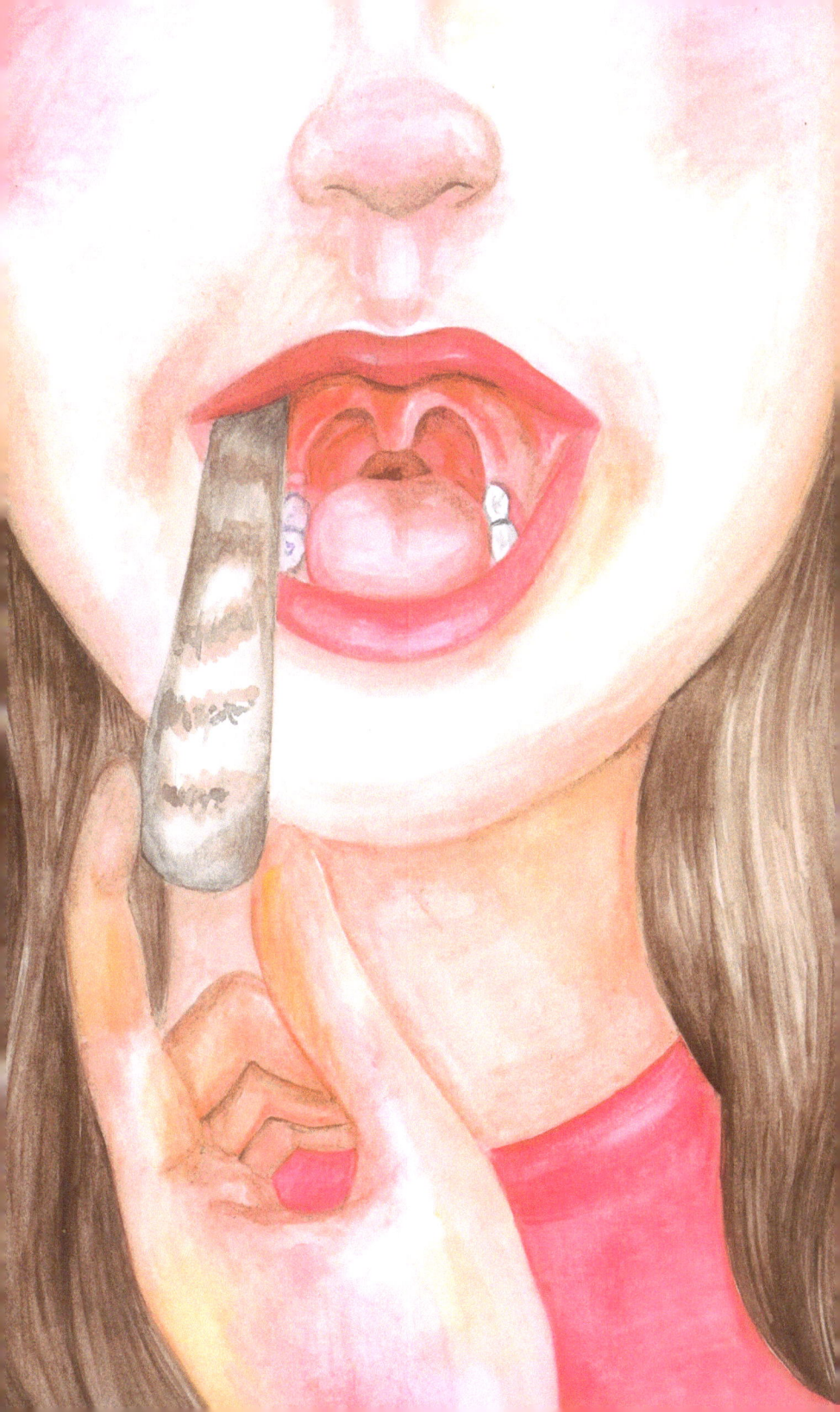

"Now Patty do chicky magic!
One chicky chew,
two chicky chew,
three chicky chew, and..."

...POOF!

Patty chewed her chicky piece right up!

And that's the story of how Picky Patty

learned not to be so picky.

From the Author

As a speech and feeding therapist I have worked with many families who were faced with significant food refusals from their little ones. I began recommending playful techniques to families to take the pressure off of eating, and saw positive changes occur—often much faster than traditional means.

My hope is that you can take the ideas from this story and the following strategies, to use as helpful tools for your child.

Lori Nachtigal Rothschild

Feeding Ideas for Picky Children

1) CREATE SHAPES OUT OF FOOD, OR USE FOODS TO REPRESENT FAMILIAR OBJECTS. Cheddar cheese bricks can be "stacking blocks," broccoli can be "little trees," and character/animal sandwiches can be made from molds. There are many commercially available molds for shapes, animals, and vehicles.

2) TRY USING PLATES AND UTENSILS WITH FUN CHARACTERS, WHILE TEACHING YOUR CHILD TO "PLAY" WITH NEW FOODS.

3) EMPHASIZE "TASTING" RATHER THAN CHEWING OR SWALLOWING. Encourage your child to lick, bite, hold, and move a food piece side-to-side in his mouth. Lessen the pressure by reassuring your child that he may spit out or remove the food piece.

4) TRY CREATING FOOD ART. There are endless ideas for colorful food art and food characters on social media. Kids are much more likely to try foods that they perceive as fun and colorful.

5) TRY "PAINTING" BY USING VEGETABLES OR FRUIT STRIPS AS PAINTBRUSHES. I like using veggies cut into French fry shapes, and pairing them with dips and spreads to use as "paint." Alternatively, make fun vegetable shapes like "circle cucumbers" or "pepper flowers" to use as "food stamps" with spreads. Move towards painting spreads onto target foods like breads, chicken, eggs, meats, and tofu.

6) USE COLORFUL, MELTABLE FOODS, OR FOODS THAT REQUIRE MINIMAL CHEWING—LIKE BISCUITS OR CEREALS. Take a small piece and place it on the center of your child's tongue. Then have your child open and close his mouth while playing "peek-a-boo" with the food piece. Encourage your child to hold the piece on his tongue for longer periods while you count. Start by counting to 5 and slowly increase the time frame.

7) SET CRITERIA FOR CHEWING NEW FOODS. FOR EXAMPLE, SAY "LET'S TRY 2 CHEWS." Let your child remove the food if he doesn't want to finish chewing or swallowing. Keep increasing exposure to the target food until he begins to fully chew and swallow.

8) MAKE A PICTURE BOOK OF FOODS YOUR CHILD EATS AND FOODS YOU WOULD LIKE YOUR CHILD TO TRY. You can download images of foods and food labels, and paste them into a "try it" book. Use a thumbs up (or thumbs up sticker) for foods he likes and a sideways thumb for foods your child is still learning to like.

9) USE A TOY OR GAME AS A REINFORCER. Every time your child licks, holds, sucks on, moves a piece (side-to-side), or chews, he then takes a turn with the toy or game.

10) USE A DIVIDED PLATE FOR CHILDREN WHO DON'T LIKE THEIR FOODS TO "TOUCH." Slowly move foods towards each other by having foods "kiss," "bump," or "crash" in to each other. Then, try having your child kiss new foods "goodbye" by placing at his lips.

11) TRY EATING TOGETHER AS A FAMILY TO ENCOURAGE MODELING, SHARING, AND TRYING FAMILY FOODS. Present foods "family style," where everybody passes and serves themselves.

12) PLAY A GAME OF HIDE AND SEEK. Hide a cereal or small food piece in your cheek pocket. While your mouth is closed, move the piece with your tongue to the other side. Then ask your child to "find the food." Your child should tap the side of your cheek with the food piece inside. Have your child then "hide the food" in his own cheek.

13) IF YOUR CHILD ONLY EATS A FEW FOODS, ADD A NEW DIMENSION TO HIS FOOD. For example, if he only eats pasta, try using pasta in different shapes, flavors, or colors.

14) SOME CHILDREN WON'T INTERACT WITH FOODS BASED ON THEIR COLOR OR APPEARANCE. Try using food coloring to make green foods less scary (i.e. dye breads and pastas green as a way to discuss green foods and make veggies less threatening).

15) WORK ON "TOUCHING" FOODS YOUR CHILD WON'T INTERACT WITH. Guide your child to "tap" the food with a spoon, "poke" with a fork, and "press" with his fingers.

16) FREEZE HEALTHY SMOOTHIES INTO ICE POPS OR ICE CUBES. Try using the ice, or ice pop, as "lipstick," and work your way towards icing the tongue. My pickiest eaters will usually allow for icing. This also helps with anterior or hypersensitive gags.

17) WHEN INTRODUCING NEW SOLIDS, TRY PROVIDING SMALL PIECES. Typically, I provide pieces that are half the nail size of an adult female pinky nail. If your child thrusts the piece out with his tongue, place on the side of his cheek pocket. Smaller pieces are more manageable and less scary for children.

18) USE LONG, THIN PIECES OF VEGETABLES, FRUITS, CHICKEN, MEATS, AND TOFU AS "SPOONS" FOR SELF-FEEDING WITH YOGURT, HUMMUS, PEANUT BUTTER, CREAM CHEESE, DRESSINGS, AND OTHER SPREADS.

19) PLAY A GAME OF "HIDING" SMALL PIECES OF MEATS, POULTRY, AND FISH IN SOUPS, AND SMALL PIECES OF FRUITS IN YOGURTS, SMOOTHIES, AND APPLESAUCE. Have your child use his spoon to go digging. Every time he finds a piece, have him try the piece in some way (i.e. kissing, licking, or holding in his mouth).

20) FOR CHILDREN WHO DON'T LIKE BEING FED, TRY PRESENTING A WHOLE PEELED FRUIT OR VEGGIE. Picky eaters, who are teething, often enjoy gnawing on a cold vegetable or fruit. Alternatively, you can present long, thin, French fry-shaped pieces, which are easy to self-feed.

Always supervise to make sure your child doesn't gnaw off pieces that are too large to manage.

About the Author

Lori Nachtigal Rothschild has a master's degree in Speech-Language Pathology from Teachers College, Columbia University. She has over 20 years of experience addressing speech and feeding challenges in young children. This is her first book.

About the Illustrator

Alexandra Feder is a budding young artist who spends much of her time cultivating different styles of art. She is currently getting her Bachelor of Fine Arts in studio art.

www.ingramcontent.com/pod-product-compliance
Lightning Source LLC
Chambersburg PA
CBHW040347060426
42445CB00029B/37